# COPYWRITING MASTERY

## EXACTLY HOW TO BECOME A PROFESSIONAL COPYWRITING EXPERT & CREATE CONTENET THAT GETS ATTENTION & SELLS

Copyright 2014 by ClydeBank Media - All Rights Reserved.

This document is geared towards providing exact and reliable information in regards to the topic and issue covered. The publication is sold with the idea that the publisher is not required to render accounting, officially permitted, or otherwise, qualified services. If advice is necessary, legal or professional, a practiced individual in the profession should be ordered.

From a Declaration of Principles which was accepted and approved equally by a Committee of the American Bar Association and a Committee of Publishers and Associations. In no way is it legal to reproduce, duplicate, or transmit any part of this document in either electronic means or in printed format. Recording of this publication is strictly prohibited and any storage of this document is not allowed unless with written permission from the publisher.

The information provided herein is stated to be truthful and consistent, in that any liability, in terms of inattention or otherwise, by any usage or abuse of any policies, processes, or directions contained within is the solitary and utter responsibility of the recipient reader. Under no circumstances will any legal responsibility or blame be held against the publisher for any reparation, damages, or monetary loss due to the information herein, either directly or indirectly. Respective authors own all copyrights not held by the publisher. The information herein is offered for informational purposes solely, and is universal as so. The presentation of the information is without contract or any type of guarantee assurance.

**Trademarks**: All other trademarks are the property of their respective owners. The trademarks that are used are without any consent, and the publication of the trademark is without permission or backing by the trademark owner. All trademarks and brands within this book are for clarifying purposes only and are owned by the owners themselves, not affiliated with this document.

ClydeBank Media LLC is not associated with any organization, product or service discussed in this book. The publisher has made every effort to ensure that the information presented in this book was accurate at time of publication. All precautions have been taken in the preparation of this book. The publisher, author, editor and designer assume no responsibility for any loss, damage, or disruption caused by errors or omissions from this book, whether such errors or omissions result from negligence, accident, or any other cause.

Cover Illustration and Design: Katie Poorman, Copyright © 2014 by ClydeBank Media LLC
Interior Design: Katie Poorman, Copyright © 2014 by ClydeBank Media LLC

ClydeBank Media LLC<br>P.O Box 6561<br>Albany, NY 12206

Printed in the United States of America

Copyright © 2014<br>ClydeBank Media LLC<br>www.clydebankmedia.com<br>All Rights Reserved

ISBN-13 : 978-1502586292

# CONTENTS

| | |
|---|---|
| 7 - 9 | Introduction |
| 10 - 21 | \| 1 \| Purpose and Nature of Copy |
| 22 - 43 | \| 2 \| Styles of Copy : Tied To Function |
| 44 - 52 | \| 3 \| Research Techniques For Copy Development |
| 53 - 66 | \| 4 \| Copywriting Ethical Considerations |
| 67 - 73 | \| 5 \| Resources and Support For Copywriting |
| 74 - 75 | Conclusion |
| 76 - 92 | Preview of *Business Plan Writing Guide* |
| 93 | About ClydeBank Business |
| 94 - 96 | More Books by ClydeBank Business |

# INTRODUCTION

This book is intended as a reference text for those aspiring to write copy, or who need practical guidance on how to do so in their concrete business or personal situations. Writing sound copy requires an understanding of several salient issues, which this e-book tries to elucidate. Publishing copy is not merely a matter of uploading it onto a site or paying someone to include it in their publication. Severe repercussions are possible if the text is not up to standard or in some way offensive, either to reader sentiment or legally. Also, there are certain general (technical) principles of style that apply to virtually any copy, and these have been addressed too. The chapters in this book have relatively self-explanatory titles, and the reader should easily be able to skip to the section that is relevant to their specific needs.

Copywriting remains an area of vast creative experimentation and, at the same time, pressing commercial necessity, so besides a few basic, simple tactics, the reader should realize that improving their own writing skills will require some personal research and investigation.

That is, however, part of the enjoyment that the activity offers, and it is hoped that this introductory text will provide a solid basis in which to locate further research and practice.

In today's society, text has become an integral element of our environment. It is everywhere, and is used for a massive variety for purposes. The present phenomenon of mass literacy has enabled its use in practically every area of activity, and it is therefore of interest to examine how text is used to achieve certain aims or to make society safer or more organized.

The use of text in strategic applications is an established part of the modern industrialized economy. Some experts take the view that there are different types of text, such as informative, persuasive, or discursive. Their outlook is based on the principle that a text can be categorized according to the function that it serves (or is intended to serve). Therefore, some texts merely provide information, while others attempt to analyze and understand a targeted issue.

This book, however, exclusively discusses those texts which are employed in order to promote, advertise or otherwise bring to the attention g the public (in a positive light) a product, service or organization. This is a separate area of text production entirely, and one which requires different expertise on the part of the writer. It is no less important though, in that it is even more prevalent than the others and probably no less influential either. This book attempts a broad overview of the subject area, starting with a definition of the practice of copywriting, and then moving on to such matters as the technical questions of style and the research methodologies that copywriters make use of. A chapter has also been devoted to the ethical issues that may arise in the course of a copywriter's work. The final chapter supplies information on the copywriting industry, and how to obtain guidance and requisite material.

Whether the reader is aspiring to write copy, or they simply wish to develop a deeper understanding of how this form of writing operates in the economy, this e-book should provide them with a suitable frame of reference in approaching the subject on a more comprehensive level.

# CHAPTER ONE
*Purpose and Nature of Copy*

### *Purpose*

At its outset, a definition of copywriting may be expected to revolve around terms such as "persuasion" or "propaganda". Ordinary members of the public may assume that the basic intention of the copywriter is to persuade, encourage or otherwise coerce them into buying a certain product or supporting the targeted cause. The agenda of the copywriter is identified as such, and the target reader of the text may not see any further function in it.

However, copywriting is about far more than mere persuasion. The copywriter is required to achieve a more composite profile in the text, in order for it to be successful. It is, of course, true that sales copy is supposed to secure market share, but in order to realize that ambition, the text itself often has to incorporate other, more supplementary, elements. These are, as examples:

- Information
- Disclaimers

- Testimonials
- Statistics
- Analysis

It should therefore be obvious from the above list that copy does not only entail the writing of flowery, positive text in an effort to convince the reader to buy something. Copywriting may sometimes involve the extensive production of informative or analytical text, in support of the primary aim of promoting the targeted item or service. In some instances, this is essential tot eh welfare of the target readership, and should not be regarded as mere advertising. At other times, it merely forms part of the overarching marketing imperative, and the exact nature of the latter type of text has been discussed in Chapter 4, where its ethical implications are examined.

## *Information*

An example of an informative piece of sales copy would be one which introduces a new product to the market. In such cases, it is not enough for the copywriter simply to exhort the reader to purchase the product,. The latter is not going to know what it is, or what features it has. They maybe deeply suspicious of it, or they may have encountered negative hearsay already. Providing ample and accurate information is therefore very important, and does not even have to be done in a persuasive manner. Sometimes, the mere provision of such information is sufficient to attract and hold the attention of the reader and influence their purchasing decision.

Concerning the social responsibility of the advertising organization, as the copywriter also has to be sensitive tot he prevailing market situation or the needs of the target readership. Some products require the observance of safety precautions in their use, while others may have been discovered to be unsafe after their release into the market. At such times, the copywriter needs to be able to balance the promotional agenda with the urgent and simple requirement that the target reader is supplied with the necessary information about the product. Once again, this use of copy does not merely entail promotional content.

### *Discussion*

Then there are also discursive texts, or those which discuss an issue or product. Such texts are supposed to be neutral, in that they embark on an impartial examination of their subject matter and draw supposedly unbiased conclusions. In a market environment in which there are usually several suppliers of the same type of product, such texts may be used by copywriters in an attempt to outline the advantages oft heir specific brand over the others. This application of copywriting also requires the copywriter to maintain a delicate stance between overwriting the promotional aspect and neglecting the analytical component of their text. Readers are not so unenlightened as to be insensitive to an excessively positive conclusion about one specific brand, or, alternatively, an unjustifiably negative assessment of the others. At the same time, though, the copywriter is trying to establish the supreme desirability of the their client among the other available options on the market.

Besides this dilemma, however, the important point to note is that copy can also be used to analyze or discuss. This function may even be extrapolated into extensive literature, or scientific studies. While the veracity of such output may always be questioned by more cynical members of the target readership, it is nevertheless a source of information to the community, and at times it is not as unreliable as the public may expect. In some industries, large corporations contribute significantly to scientific research into new products, and their literature, while published under their official corporate auspices, is no less valid than that of independent or academic researchers. Other enterprises are able to represent themselves accurately as providing superior products to the market, since they genuinely have achieved that status, and a favorable analysis of the various market rivals is thus entirely factual and does not need to be be skewed in any way to promote the initiator's brand.

### *Administration*

All organizations, at times, need to make announcements of an administrative or legal nature. Sometimes, these announcements concern extremely negative developments, such as a motor vehicle that has been found to contain a defect, or the outcome of highly publicized litigation. Such material, while absolutely essential, is hardly promotional. The copywriter therefore needs to be able to accommodate that implication of the information in such a way that the organization is presented to the readership in a respectable and trustworthy style. On the other hand, the news provided by the text may not be negative at all, or may merely be a mundane administrative issue and as such has no bearing on the reputation or market profile of the text initiator per se. This application of copywriting results in a situation in which the copywriter has a direct and obvious imperative to provide precise and necessary data tot he public. Some of this data may be hazardous tot eh image of the advertising entity. Sometimes, undesirable facts are required to be broadcast, especially where litigation has made their continued concealment impossible, or where there is a genuine error in the supply of a product or service. An example would be a breach in the security of an online banking platform. The bank has no other option but to publicize the incident and provide safety guidelines to its clients, even though such publicity is going to cause a substantial decrease in public confidence in the bank and may lead to the loss of customers, or at least a curtailment of the addition of new ones.

A skilled copywriter is able to produce text in such circumstances which serves the purpose of rendering the administrative information, while at the same time projecting the organization as professional and dignified. This part of a copywriter's work is not always mentioned explicitly, in that it represents one of the most untoward situations that they are ever required to operate in. Phrases such as "damage control", "spin" or "public relations exercise" are sometimes used to describe how copywriters approach these disasters.

### *Disclaimers & Legal Text*

Some products and services require that they are advertised in conjunction with certain specific legal terms or text. This additional material may be stipulated by law, and as such it cannot be omitted, since such omission may expose the advertising entity to legal action or liability for compensatory damages. Copywriters always need to be aware of the legal environment in which they are operating, and this issue has been more fully addressed in Chapter 4, which deals with the ethics of the trade.

However, legal terminology is not always understandable to the target readership. Lawyers are notorious for using language, both in vocabulary and in style, in such a way that ordinary members of the public are unable to determine what they are referring, or to ascertain the exact implications of the texts that they produce. Copywriters need to be aware of this limitation in legal language (or "legalese"). They need to present the legal information in such a way that it is accessible to their readers, without detracting from its importance or semantic content.

## *The Nature of Copywriting*

Copywriters do not only write advertisements. The nature of their expertise, especially in how they exploit language in pursuit of strategic objectives, enables them to be employed in other spheres of activity. Any text that serves some underlying purpose (whether ulterior or otherwise, since it isn't necessarily so) lies within the scope of their profession. It may be a surprise to the reader to discover that many prominent public figures, such as politicians, do not, in fact, produce their own material. The speeches that state officials or corporate representatives, such as the president of the country or the CEO of a large enterprise, deliver on a regular basis are often not their own work. The fact that copywriters are able to adapt their trade to different environments and applications indicates that there are certain specific skills which they possess. These skills are inherent to the nature of the copywriting process, and as such that nature should be discussed in order to emphasize what proficiencies a copywriter should master and how they should deploy them.

The primary aim of any copywriting is to advance a deliberate agenda. This definition is the stable, most simple one on which this entire e-book is based, and the reader should be aware of it at all times. Note that it has to aspects: that the copywriter subscribes to an agenda or pre-determined cause, and, secondly, that they they do so deliberately. The deliberate nature of this loyalty is important. Writers who unintentionally or inadvertently promote a cause or product are not writing copy – they are potentially producing misguided or prejudiced trash, and they are engaged in an extremely dangerous occupation. However, this has been discussed more completely in Chapter 4. It suffices to say at present that the writer should always, but always, be entirely aware of the entire import of their text, something which may become more difficult to accomplish where they are trying to provide premeditated support for cause or organization. To the extent that copywriters have this approach, which is sometimes stated on their part, they employ a style that is appropriate to the nature of the exercise. That nature is now analyzed here.

To start with, it is unavoidably more creative, or less formally regulated, than other types of text. Copywriting requires a certain degree of creative ability to execute successfully. This is a requirement that is associated the imperative to draw the attention of the target readership and to hold it. The writer needs to be able to provoke the readership on a constructive basis, into paying attention tot he text and responding to it, hopefully in the desired manner.

Ordinarily, people seek out the texts that they need and then examine them, such as a student researching an assignment topic. The writers of such material therefore have no need to enhance its appeal or render it as provocative because those who require it will make their own attempt to locate it. Promotional text, in contrast, is typically in competition with many similar texts, in a market environment which is host to several rival product offerings. Copywriters are not merely trying to supply the target market with information, or to raise awareness.

They need to approach the readership in such a way that they also attract attention to their texts.

There are various techniques in use to achieve this aim. These are techniques of writing that can be taught, and practiced, and some of them even have specific titles, in the same way that standard or traditional internal structures in music also have their own unique identifying names. Chapter 5 provides more information on how to obtain resource or training material, for those who want to up-skill themselves, or expand their existing acumen. The important implication here is that copywriting is not the preserve of artistic geniuses or immensely talented poets. Indeed, such attributes are of assistance in copywriting, as they are in any writing task, but the are not prerequisite to success in the industry. This is because of certain other factors which a good copywriter should be sensitive to, and which are now discussed in the next few paragraphs. One of them is that economic or commercial aspect of the industry. Copywriters are not producing text in the abstract hope that at some point in time, someone will read it and then, even more hopefully, that the reader is actually going to react positively to the text. The purpose of the text is not entertainment or provocation, although these may be secondary objectives in support of the primary one, which is the intentional advancement of the product, service or entity in the advertisement, as stated above.

As an exercise in strategic writing, successful copywriting therefore does not rely entirely on the beauty or originality of the text, so much as how effectively it accesses the target market. Memorable advertising exhibits an acute propensity to capture and retain the emotional and intellectual energy of the targeted reader. The intelligent manipulation of that reader's sensitivities, loyalties and concerns is sometimes more important than the creativity or "artistic flair" displayed in the text.

This, necessitates an astute awareness of the market environment in which the copy is going to be used. Copywriters need to understand exactly who they are writing for, and why. They need to research their target market, the history of what they are advertising, and all the salient issues associated with both of those, in or. They also need to have an adequate understanding of marketing, how it happens, how it is made more effective, and then, in turn, how text can be employed to maximum effect in its processes. In short, the copywriter is not merely a writer. They are a marketer.

This is the opposite approach of many purely creative writers, who simply deposit their text into the public domain and then await a response. Some genres or readerships have been initiated in that way, just as "breakthrough" albums in the music industry have had a similar impact. Many creative writers, such as novelists, do not always identify a finite target readership for their work. They may not even have the assumption that anyone "out there" is going to pay any attention to it. Yet their text is highly original, and pleasant to read. Artistically, it is impressively accomplished. But it is utterly useless as promotional material. It has no underlying intention and it does not focus on anyone in particular in the population.

This is in stark contrast to copywriting, where the text is supposed to provoke or elicit positive action in the target readership. They are not merely supposed to view or appreciate the text – they are further supposed to engage in some concrete activity associated with it, such as the purchase of a product or the overt support of a cause. Creative writers, on the other hand, anticipate only the reader's aesthetic or intellectual appreciation of the text itself. That is the primary intention of the text – to function as entertainment or art. There is often no secondary agenda. Copywriters have the inverse approach; they may use aesthetic appeal, or they may not, but their primary objective is the promotional aspect of their text.

### Summary

This chapter has attempted to explain the nature of copywriting and the various purposes that it may be used for. The primary definition provided here, that copywriting is the production of text in the deliberate promotion of an identified cause or commercial item (deliberate in that the writer is aware of their promotion of the latter), should be remembered at all times throughout the rest of this book. The overarching objective of copywriting is to secure market share for the advertiser. Copywriters are therefore not the same as solely creative writers, or authors of informative texts, in that they are trying to bring about a commercial response in the target readership. The ultimate aim of their text is to generate sales, or to cause some other positive, concrete reaction. This principle too, should not be lost sight of as the reader progresses through the rest of this book.

Aspiring copywriters, or those who need to enter the trade in order to promote their own enterprises, should not automatically assume that they do not have the necessary literary talent to produce effective texts. Copywriters, as a rule, have tertiary qualifications these days, and not only in writing. Training is available, and experience serves to improve the skills of new writers. Chapter 5 lists more substantially how to approach the development of such skills, and how to locate resources that may be of assistance in that regard.

# CHAPTER TWO
*Styles of Copy : Tied To Function*

Different genres of literature require different approaches from those who operate within them. The nature of the genre determines how the writer uses language, and what vocabulary they rely on to structure in their texts. Copywriting makes is open to certain techniques and stylistic devices which may be mostly alien to other genres, and as such they should be mastered by or at least familiar to anyone who entertains aspirations of writing effective copy. These elements of style have been listed below under broad descriptive headings. The analysis and classification of text, or text types and their subsidiary structural components, is an entire academic subject field, and various scholars may subscribe to their own preferred systems of definition. The categories included in this chapter are not, therefore, always standard, and the terms used may be assigned or classed differently by other authors.

### *Register*

Register is, in fact, a term in linguistics which refers to the way that language is used in relation to a specific target readership (or audience, since it applies equally to spoken language). Register defines the diction (choice of words or vocabulary), the type of language used, and how it is deployed. For example, in everyday situations we encounter slang, casual chat, formal speeches business communication, scientific or academic literature, and ordinary, plain language such as that used by newsreaders. All of these situations require a different register, or endemic use of language. The copywriter needs to be able to express salient information and the marketing imperative in any register. They can't anticipate who they are going to be writing for, so they need to be able to master any register in the language that they are using. For example, writing copy for teenagers may involve the use of high school slang, something which the writer may not be entirely familiar with (or at all). Writing an advertisement for retiring middle-aged upper-class professionals, on the other hand, requires an entirely different linguistic presentation. Appropriate register is important, because it enables the target readership to access the material. This is not merely concerned with mutual intelligibility, i.e. whether they are able to under5tand what the advertiser is saying. The use of known terms, such as slang words, instantly attracts the reader's attention. The cliché is that the writer approaches the reader "on their own level". Readers who use the deployed register will take such material seriously, even if they do not always agree with its content or show any further interest in the advertised item.

However, register is also significant in that it serves to identify the target market. A product that has a broader potential reach than one market segment may be hampered in its popularity by the use of an exclusive register. Using the examples above, of the teenage school-kids and the retiring professionals, a product that is relevant to both groups may not attain prominence among one or the other, if it is advertised in only one register. In fact, register can encourage aversion in other parts of the economy. The use of slang may cause people who do not use it to feel excluded, or even antagonistic towards the advertiser. Polished, formal language, too, may alienate younger readers, or those less educated. Register also has the ability to damage or improve the image of the advertiser, in that it should be appropriate to that image. A traditionally respectable institution such as a bank, for example, may be criticized for using street slang in its advertising. An inappropriate register detracts from the image of the advertiser, regardless of the merits of the market offering. Some consumers may even select a rival supplier purely on that basis, since they are unable to reconcile their own personal image with what the advertiser is projecting to the market. If the target readership cannot identify themselves as the target of the material, at least partially, they are unlikely to respond positively to it, or even pay attention to it.

In determining which register to use, the writer should make a proper assessment of market research, as it relates to the target market. In this exercise, the input of the client is essential. The client needs to be specify who they are aiming their market offering at. They should be able to provide the writer with a theoretical profile of their average customer. Alternatively, the writer should be able to compose such a profile themselves. If they are not informed as to the language that the target market uses, they should research it until they are able to use it themselves to a passable degree. An error in diction is lethal to the success of the material.

**Text Function**

This is another extremely broad heading. It was introduced in the previous chapter (Chapter 1), and it refers to the way that different texts have different functions. The same text can have more than one function at the same time, so the advertising imperative in sales copy is sometimes served by other, subsidiary roles, such as the provision of information or entertainment. Exactly how these roles complement each other in the eventual text is an issue that he writer needs to resolve at the outset. Sometimes, the composition of the text is determined by the nature of the marketing exercise. A new product is advertised in two ways: by trying to draw as much attention to it as possible, and through the provision of extensive information about its specifications and performance. Older, more established items require less informative text, and more incentive to use them, especially where they are competing with rival brands in a saturated market. Some products are so popular, or so traditionally entrenched in consumer purchasing patterns, that their advertising literally requires no text at all. As a general principle, the more obscure or specialized a product or service is, the more text it requires. Material aimed at highly qualified or very discerning consumers, such as state-of-the-art medical equipment or high-level art, is usually introduced using copious descriptive text, most of which is not necessarily styled to be positive. In contrast, very prominent items, such as soft-drink brands or fast-food chains, can be advertised merely with a picture and an emblem.

In deciding on which functions a text should serve, the writer needs to answer the obvious question: what is this text supposed to do? Sales copy is always supposed to generate sales (and interest in the market generally), so the other possible functions of the text are then structured around this primary one. In this way, the copy is strategically designed before it is written, so as to maximize its impact on the target readership.

### *Spin*

Spin is a jargon term which refers to how writers try to shape or modify the reader's perception of an issue or item. The term "spin" is often used in connection with political figures, but it also has application in everyday language. The common expression "to put a positive/negative spin" on something denotes how people may use language to make something sound better (or worse) than it really is. Advertisers are notorious for doing this, and the client may even insist on it. They try to portray their market offering ass the supreme option available, and they may also try to persuade the target market that they are not sensible if they choose another. Anyone who tries to write copy is going to encounter this issue at some stage, so they should be aware of how copywriters accommodate it. One possible temptation is to generate as much positive sentiment as possible in the material, and entirely omit anything which may be perceived as negative by the reader. This is not uncommon, but then it is only available as a strategy to the copywriter where it is permitted, both by law and by the target market. The risk involved in this approach is that some "advantages" of the item may actually be regarded as defects by the target readership, or may not be regarded as important. An example would be a magnetic keyring. Material advertising the keyring may include a loud announcement of its magnetism as an important feature. Some consumers, though, may have the opinion that he magnet makes selecting the right key more awkward, and is therefore an irritating nuisance, or that the principle of using a mere magnet as a keyring is too hazardous to tolerate. The writer should assess carefully whether a feature is genuinely worth emphasizing, or whether it should simply be stated in a list among the others.

Spin can also be excessive. Every so often, a politician becomes embroiled in a scandal, and their spokesperson then embarks on a procession of scarcely plausible statements in an attempt to limit the repercussions for their employer. target market should be assumed to be highly intelligent, at all times. This is especially so because they are expected to use their money in response to the advertisement. A purchasing decision may be of immense significance to the reader, so the writer should never attempt deception, or try to manipulate the target reader so severely that they experience the attempt as offensive.

It should also be stated that spin is sometimes destructive to the purpose of generating sales. Expert consumers, such as the medical professionals referred to in a previous section of this chapter, will not appreciate overdriven claims or redundant garbage in the advertising material that they receive. Such consumers are far more likely to respect neutrality, since they are guaranteed to buy the advertised item and their choice is merely as to which brand. They are able to assess the performance of the item far better than the copywriter, so trying too hard to persuade them to purchase a specific brand is a waste of time, and the suspicion that it elicits may even result in blatant aversion. The writer should be extremely cautious about resorting to negative spin. Negative spin is used to discourage consumers from opting for other brands. This is a dangerous angle in advertising, because it can be pursued to an excessive extent, in which case the other band(s) may have recourse to preventive legal action. A fairly common occurrence in marketing arises where one brand suspects that they are being referred to obliquely in the material of another. Writers should always be sensitive to this aspect oft heir text, as the legal implications can be substantial. Generally, negative spin is not desirable, since it may consolidate existing support for the advertiser but also have that same effect on consumers loyal to the other brand. The latter may perceive that their initial choice of product or service is being questioned, i.e. that their judgment as the customer is being criticized, and this may antagonize them into avoiding the advertiser entirely.

### *Attracting Attention*

In order to be of any use at all, marketing material has to achieve this aim. It needs to be noticed and inspected by the target market. The initial attraction of attention is therefore one of its primary intentions. How writers achieve this is determined to some extent by the overall layout or design of the material. Sometimes, the writer can rely on explosive graphic supplementation to assist the text, such as vivid color, massive fonts and interesting layout strategies. At other times, the semantic impact of the text itself is all they have to capture and hold the reader's attention. The effect of graphic material won't be discussed here, since this e-book deals primarily with writing per se. turning to the use of language to gain attention, there are several tactics that are available to he copywriter. These are listed below. This is not an exhaustive list, and should not be regarded as such.

- Use unusual or extreme words, such as millionaire or razzmatazz.
- State an absurd or or drastic concept, such as "You could be the next Rihanna" or "Apples are free tomorrow".

- Use a striking question, such as "Are you happy with your weight?" or "What's your favorite color?"
- Introduce an already prominent name (this requires the permission of that person, which may be extremely hard or impossible/expensive to obtain, since they are required to endorse the advertised item.
- Quote a famous person, which requires no permission, but then you need to be sure that they are regarded at least neutrally by the target market. Using the wrong person can backfire horrifically.
- Use an imperative, "Save your pennies!" or "Cut those carbs!"
- Indicate that the material provides previously hidden or sensitive information, such as "The truth about..." or "Here's what you've been missing..."
- Make a striking statement, by a satisfied customer like "I saved 20% on my insurance premiums in two years."
- Hi-jack a current (trending) news item. It may not even have anything whatsoever to do with the material itself, but it is sure to catch the eye of passing consumers. "Make Mom your candidate in this election."

At all times, the writer should seek to avoid offensive or excessively strident headlines. They are seen as immature and they crate an unprofessional, negative impression. Expletives are entirely out of line. Sensitive issues, such as sex or the death penalty, should also be avoided. A headline such as "Orgasm in these sneakers" or "If we're out of stock, shoot the asshole who grabbed the last one" are unacceptable and won't be approved by your client or the target market, no matter how humorous or sensational they may seem.

*Format*

Format is the term used to describe how the text is packaged visually. It is sometimes referred to as the layout, either of text or the advertisement. Understandably, some people may think that format only refers to the text formatting, but in advertising the visual impact of the material relies on far more than the mere manipulation of fonts or paragraph styles. Of course, the writer cannot or does not participate to any significant extent in the graphic design of the material. That is an entirely separate sphere of professional activity, and graphic designers have separate qualifications and expertise. There are those who provide both services tot heir clients, but generally speaking people are specialized in either one or the other discipline.

Having said as much, it behoves the copywriter to be well versed in contemporary formatting techniques and aids. Their knowledge of word processing software needs to be at least intermediate, if not advanced. Some clients insist on a certain standardized style, or use an in-house style-book, sot he writer should be able to comply with the instructions in that regard. For example, if the client insists that a piece is written in Times New Roman, font size 12, with headings, would you realize that you have been reading text matching those specifications the entire time in this book? However, formatting of a text entail much more than mere font selection. Texts which include a large amount of material, such as documentary texts or product manuals, may require extensive formatting using a range of techniques. There are two very important characteristics of a text's format that the writer needs to keep under control:

- It must be entirely functional
- It must be uniform

The writer therefore needs to know how to address more complex situations, such as bulleted lists, page layout (for example, the insertion of pictures and relevant backgrounds), and the uniform and tidy editing of the text generally. This is part of the impression that the text creates, and can be utilized in attracting the reader's attention and providing them with a pleasant reading experience. To this end, different formatting devices can be used to approach different target markets or subject areas. Writing for medical practitioners would not allow for the use of more casual fonts like woodplank or the handwriting imitations. On the other hand, a relatively more slangy advertisement might not even use a standard font, but resort to actual handwritten text. Copywriters need to be sensitive to how text formatting is received psychologically by their target readership.

```
Let us use a simple example. This paragraph
has been typed in a different font, Courier. It
```

appears more old-fashioned and less professional. Maybe you are already asking yourself: why didn't they use a more "modern" font in this book? How old is this text? When was it originally created? It feels like it was made on one of the first 1990's computers.

**Or the author could have used this one, but this is too heavy. It's too pretentious. Too individualist. It isn't as practical and does not function well as a "body copy" typeface. It uses more ink and it's style is very distinct. You could use this as a display font on a concert program or on a local flyer perhaps. There's a reason why it's named Impact.**

This aspect of the material's layout obviously has an effect on the literary style of the text itself. In some instances, it may be helpful to the copywriter to liaise with the graphic designer in an attempt to maximize the synergy between the two disciplines. This is not always possible, and so the writer also needs to be able to adapt their textual expression to existing graphic material or the overarching concept of the advertisement as specified by the client.

### *Other Micro-Structural Tactics*

The micro-structure of a text is its innate, internal structure and format. These are related to the practical use of language, in sometimes small yet highly important ways. Some of the may seem petty or inconsequential to the inexperienced writer, but they are available nonetheless. Some writers may also object to some of them , or state a preference for others, so the reader needs to decide for themselves what they are prepared to accept in their texts, or what their experience shows them is viable. Aspiring writers should also remember that there is no hard and fasts rule as to what is effective and what isn't. That is why, essentially, writing is almost always a creative process, on some level at least. Experimentation, experience, and a sustained focus on the project objective should ensure that in time the writer develops the necessary skills and, even more importantly, the ability to determine when and how to use them.

### *Hit Them With The Headline*

People may associate this principle more closely with reporting, such as in newspapers or on news sites. However, sales copy also needs to include a conspicuous entry line, one that catches the eye of the reader and makes them interested in examining the rest of the material. Naturally, the formatting of the ad headline isn't usually the same as the rest of the text, and there are various techniques in use in generating sharp, memorable lines. Some of these involve the use of a question, the use of expletives, an absurd statement, or a sensational piece of information. Writers who are studying how to improve their composition of headlines or leading text should pay attention to the literature on journalistic practice and newspaper editing, since news sub-editors are past masters in this area and their insights are extremely valuable. After all, the entire purpose of a newspaper is to be sold, and sometimes the headline on the front page is the only aspect of the publication that is necessary to ensure that outcome.

### *Statistics & Data*

These are the (supposedly) hared facts and figures that support the instruction to buy the advertised item. Usually, they may be regarded as very persuasive, since they are immutable and the reader cannot argue with them. However, they need to be applied sensibly, otherwise they may have the converse effect. Copywriters should make sure that the statistics they use are, in fact, convincing. Simple math can expose some stats as utter trash or as the result of misleading interpretation. An example is the advertisement for a luxury soap that contained the line "with a quarter percent moisturizing cream". It is not clear from this line whether the soap is composed of 25% cream, or 0.25%. people are also inherently untrusting of statistics, and so an isolated, very generalized figure, such as "50% of people" is hazardous and may cause aversion to the rest of the material. Any data and statistics may seem more concrete if they are accompanied by a citation, such as the name of the researcher who formulated them or the institution that published them.

### *Superlatives*

Use sparingly. Superlative language involves the use of intensifying adjectives and descriptive terms. This is an obvious tactic in sales copy,. But sometimes it can be excessive. Describing a product as "the best in the world" is not persuasive and does nothing to encourage reader appreciation. But the line "a market leader in our country" is much harder to reject.

*Omission, Not Inclusion* – it's in what you don't say

Sometimes, advertisers omit information about their product from the marketing material this information is either entirely known already, or it is negative to the image of the item. Advertisers should be circumspect about what they include in their material. The proviso here, though, is that the material should contain the information that is legally required. Trying to hide weak points about the advertised matter is sometimes illegal, or may lead to consumers boycotting it entirely once they realize that they have not been adequately informed. Excessive use of omission can also arouse the suspicion of the reader, since they may speculate as to why certain details are missing, or whether there is a "catch".

*Start With & Emphasize The Best Point*

I keeping with this approach of isolating the favorable points about the item, one tactic is to start the material by mentioning its best aspect(s). these are then repeatedly raised throughout the material, instead of listing a more comprehensive range of points.

***Shorter, Not Longer*** – simple, short paragraphs

Sales copy needs to be compact. It should be concise. There are usually other advertisers in the same market sector, and much advertising is positioned where it cannot be perused for a long period of time. Consumers are also notoriously fickle in how they devote their attention. As an example, internet users spend only about 7 seconds on a site, unless it it provides them with what they are looking for. It is impossible to examine the entire package of content and supplementary advertising on a modern website in that space of time.

***Don't Be Pretentious***

Copywriters may enjoy working with language, and they may even regard themselves as especially talented in this activity. However, intricate or contrived language structures are not appreciated, no matter whether they are intended to be humorous or intelligent. If a joke is going to be used, it should be succinct and genuinely funny. Humor also has the potential to insult people. The use of rare or sophisticated language in an attempt to impress the reader is also risky, since they may experience the material as condescending and avoid it entirely. Register is determined by the target market and the writer should always remember that principle.

***Ask "Yes" Questions***

Another tactic in engaging the target reader is to introduce questions into the text. It may be advantageous if these are answered with "yes" instead of "no". How often have we seen the response to an advertisement that, as soon as a question is asked, the consumer says "no" emphatically and changes the TV channel or throws the magazine aside? "No" questions are, in that sense, not advisable and should be used with caution. This response may be completely unsubjective, in that the reader may genuinely believe that the material does not apply to them. Insightful, searching questions are a method of attracting and retaining reader attention, and so their use is a viable technique in copywriting and one which the writer should consider.

### *Interrogate The Subjunctive*

For those whose high school grammar lessons were not a priority, the subjunctive is the part of speech which enables possible or imaginary (future) actions to be expressed. The most common words in the English language used in the subjunctive are could, should and would. However, the entire concept is based on nonexistent or potential actions and developments. One philosophy in copywriting is that material should not contain the subjunctive. According to this approach, the reader should not be told that a product "might be" satisfactory. They should not be told that they "may" enjoy its use. Rather, concrete, finite verbs should be used, such as "will" or "shall". However, this is not always possible, since some claims as to product performance may be tested on legal grounds and opposed. In some instances, the subjunctive actually preempts litigation, so its use is not as noxious as some commentators may assert. An example is where the performance of a product is described as totally exceptional or of astonishing proportions. The disclaimer (which is sometimes present in smaller text) is that the product may only achieve that performance under certain very preferential circumstances. It is illegal to state that the user will definitely experience that level of performance. Another example is the way that supermarkets advertise raw ingredients in prepared form, in photos of ready meals, complete with crockery and garnish. The standard term in such material, namely "serving suggestion", is a not-so-subtle use of the subjunctive principle. It indicates what the reader may be able to accomplish with the ingredients, and not what they'll automatically turn out to be.

### *Encourage A Concrete Reaction*

The purpose of sales copy is to generate sales. It is not enough for the reader to examine the material and abandon it without changing their consumer behavior. They should either choose the advertised item, or at least inform others of it or assume a positive attitude towards it. The material should therefore target these outcomes and should be structured appropriately. One possible method of pursuing such consequences it to insert a specific instruction into the text. The readers is then told to do something. This instruction may not necessarily be to buy or use the advertised item, but it may be an imperative in support of that objective. One insurance ad, published some years ago, finished with the instruction to cut out the ad, fill in the reader's personal details, and post it to the advertiser. The line "But be careful, those scissors are sharp" was in keeping with the warning tone of the entire text, and was an attempt to reinforce the point that life is unpredictable and hazardous and that insurance is therefore necessary. Ending an advertisement with an instruction, whether to buy or something other action, encourages the reader to assimilate the text more completely and to modify their economic activities according to its imperative.

### *Summary*

Copy is sometimes burdened with vague descriptions such as "beautiful", attractive", striking or "high-impact". Clients sometimes include these terms in their briefs, and the writer may feel daunted in trying to attain them. However, the marketing environment is notoriously exaggerated in its use of language, and sometimes in its expectations too. The writer should never be discouraged by poorly defined or seemingly unreasonable project descriptions. Ultimately, even the best copy cannot guarantee the desired sales, and the internal troubles of the client enterprise may be more responsible for the failure of an advertising campaign than the material used in the later. At the same time, writers should be cautious about future relations with clients who repeatedly reject material or who remain averse to providing a more detailed, specific brief. If the client cannot or will not pin down an exact description of what they want, what they are trying to achieve int heir target market or who the text is aimed at, the writer should inform them politely that the success of the text may be prejudiced by this absence of information. See Chapter 4 for more advice on how to handle consistently vague or uncooperative clients. To finish this chapter, here are five basic guidelines in copywriting. These have been composed by the author, and they are not always listed in order of importance. There are so many philosophies and strategies in the industry that it is pointless trying to name all of them, and the reader should realize that they are no less qualified through their experience to formulate their own guidelines, as they progress in their career.

*1. Make The Text Memorable*

Sales copy can potentially use entertainment or artistry as an aspect, in an attempt to attract attention to it or to reinforce its message. Some advertising is remembered solely on that basis. The music or art of the material is retained by society as exceptional in its own right, and the original advertiser or product is not considered as important, even generations later. The copywriter is able to broadcast material of that nature to their audience, and it pays to give your target readership something to remember. It is, of course, also good for sales, since it obviously improves the chances of success of the material generally.

*2. Respect The Target Reader*

this is one area where register and data integrity are so important. Building trust in a brand is essential, and inaccurate information, misleading statements or inappropriate use of language destroys that potential relationship. Also, excessive efforts to coerce the reader into compliance with the instructions in the material, whether to agree with an attitude or to purchase a product, may be deemed as offensive.

### 3. Product, Not Packaging

This point follows from the preceding one. Never assume that your target reader is an idiot and that they'll believe any trash you put out there. This is not merely a pragmatic consideration. Deception is not appreciated, will not result in consistent or sustainable sales, and may even provoke official sanction. At the same time, what passes as deception may be interpreted differently by the writer and their audience. The former should therefore understand how drastic they can make their use of superlative language or their coercive sentiments. Spin needs to be adjusted or omitted in response to the nature and attitude of the target market.

### 4. Other Brands Don't Exist

Brand rivalry is an important element in marketing, but advertising material should not focus on other brands. Never give them any attention, unless the advertised brand is genuinely and palpably the market leader. Even then, it is still not regarded as mature or healthy to spend more time criticism someone else's enterprise than promoting your own. Think of a sports coach being interviewed before a match. What do they do? Does they spend their time trying to degrade the other team? Or do they talk up his own? If another brand is defective or involved in a scandal, you do not need to use your client's resources to sponsor the negative publicity. There will be enough of that in the public domain anyway. Don't mention it, or try to aggravate it.

*5. Pull The Trigger*

Sales copy is, after all, a marketing exercise. So, aim fort the sale. Target the business. Engage with the reader and try to generate interest in the advertised item. Always remember the primary aim – to generate revenue through the promotion of the advertised matter.

# CHAPTER THREE
*Research Techniques For Copy Development*

Part of any professional writing is the conduct of research. Hard-hitting, high-impact texts usually require the inclusion of relevant information which may be of use to the target readership or which is likely to attract their attention. Sometimes this information is able to cause that effect, and at other times it needs to be packaged in such a way that its importance is emphasized. Regardless of its nature it sometimes lies beyond the experience of the writer, and they need to evaluate it so as to provide an effective text to their client.

This chapter discusses various methods of conducting such research, and also outlines the potential problems associated with each. The reader should note that no one method is always applicable to any given project, and they need to determine which is the most appropriate based on the nature of the project and the availability of information in different media. It should be added that a diversity of sources usually leads to a more stable, irrefutable base of knowledge to draw on in writing the eventual text.

### *The Internet*

These days, the internet is an obvious starting point for any research. Search engines make the rapid retrieval of extensive information very easy, and there are usually many sites dedicated to any given topic. The convenience of the medium also encourages it uses by the entire range of those who participate in research, such as scholars, academics, writers, or even prisoners. However, there are certain points to remember in using the internet for this purpose. At times, the internet is, in effect, the enemy of the writer (or the researcher), and as such it should be used with caution in serious, professional writing work. Indiscriminate use of this medium can have a negative impact on the quality of the text, or cause an adverse response among the target readership.

To start with, it is impossible to ascertain the veracity of the material on many sites on the internet. There is no universal authority online, and there is no standard of publication either. Anything is allowed, and little, if anything, is verified by anyone else. To the extent that writers use the internet as a source of information, they therefore need to be able to assess (and disqualify) material in a sensible fashion. The following are some important tips on how to approach online material. Who is the author? This is easy to determine. The first aspect of the material to examine is the site it appears on. Is the site established, and has it been so for a relatively long period of time? How reputable is this site? As to the author themselves, who are they? Are they a recognized expert in the industry they are publishing in? Titles such as

"Doctor" or "Professor" are not persuasive in answering this question. Anyone can assume those titles online. However, they cannot establish a professional profile in the same way. Sometimes, putting a name through a simple search engine inquiry can reveal exactly who they are, where they practice, and whether they are worth taking seriously, especially where they have been linked to past controversy or they have been expelled form their stated profession. Perhaps, there are possible issues of professional loyalty, such as alternative health practitioners who subscribe to questionable therapy techniques and then enthusiastically promote them online.

### *Impartiality Vs. Neutrality*

Is the information corroborated by at least one or two other sources? How extreme is the information or opinion expressed in the material? Is this an opinion that is shared by others in the same industry? How easy is it to find other authors who support or agree with this information?

In the quest for neutrality, it is sometimes tempting to make use of only certain sites, which are then regarded as irreproachable, and always accurate. However, this is a trap that writers should be aware of. There are no such sites online, unless they are specific, dedicated sites in a particular industry, in which case copywriters in that industry should take the time to research and record therm for future reference. Note that impartiality does not equate to neutrality. Facts may be correct without being complete, or may only support one angle in a contested debate. An example of a site that is potentially open to abuse in all of these ways is Wikipedia. Wikipedia is a free online encyclopedia. However, as the "wiki" part of the name indicates, it is maintained by its user community (that is, essentially, what the term wiki refers to, in any context). Although Wikipedia does have a core support staff, it is mainly populated with text written by voluntary writers, and users are able to comment on the text or suggest revisions. This has sometimes led to rather public incidents in the past, where pages on controversial or despised public figures, for example, have been doctored to reflect extremely negative, sometimes flagrantly abusive, sentiments. The pages can be updated at any time, so it may be several days before more sympathetic users realize the transgression and rectify the offending content. In the 2007 Rugby World Cup, customary tournament favorites New Zealand were eliminated in the quarter-final by France, who scored a decisive try (similar to a touchdown in American Football) after what New Zealand supporters alleged was a forward pass (an illegal movement in rugby). In rugby, it is the duty of the referee to detect and penalize such illegal plays. The referee of that match, Wayne Barnes, was subsequently subjected to a savage attack on his Wikipedia page. As one rogue user stated, Barnes was "lynched in 2007 by a mob with 20/20 vision", even though there was no basis in reality for this assertion, and Barnes was still very much alive. However, the addition of inaccurate information to the site is possible in the other direction too, in that a page may contain embellished or falsely complimentary data, or may exclude contested or negative facts entirely, as their daily users, who are loyal to the subject of the page, may not allow such facts to be published at all.

The principle of user revision is dangerous to professional writers. Prominent figures obviously make an effort to edit their information so that it appears in the most favorable light possible, and some pages are updated on a daily basis. The writers on Wikipedia are not professionally affiliated with the site an, nor are they experts in the subjects that they write on. Some of them openly state that they have had thousands of pages published on the site. This is not as impressive as it may seem, since the quality of all that text, and the depth of its insight, cannot possibly be as significant as one may desire, and definitely not as substantial as a professional writer requires. In fact, experience has shown that there is no 100% consistent factual integrity on the site. There are sometimes glaring conflicts between the information provided and that published on other sites, such as subject-specific ones. As a simple exercise, the reader is advised to use Wikipedia as a reference in a few projects, and then to make a point of juxtaposing the information that it provides with other, more specialized sources. The results may be alarming. As a basic starting point to research, Wikipedia is a moderate success. As a cursory introduction to a new topic, perhaps. As a source of primary facts for school assignments, maybe. But as an in-depth, comprehensive research resource for a professional writer, it is not recommended.

## *Market Research*

This is essential to a marketing campaign, and is usually sponsored by the client themselves. The purpose of market research is to establish who is interested in the product or service, who they are, and what their opinion is of it. This is information that, as stated in Chapter 1, is simply indispensable to the copywriter. They typically have to write their text based on an identified target readership, so where a company may refer to the market, the writer understands the reader of the advertising material. Market research can, however, may be susceptible to flaws or destructive techniques. In assessing any such research, the writer should always be able to determine its potential value to their task, by taking into account the following factors.

- **What is the research sample?** This is a simple matter of mathematics. Questions need to be answered, such as how large the sample is (or how small).
- **Who does it consist of?** Are the people targeted by the researchers likely to be interested in the advertised item? Do they represent the entire possible target market? Inclusivity is very important in advertising material, so market research should give an adequate indication as to whom the copywriter is writing for.
- **How was the sample gathered?** There are several methods of researching the market, and some of them are not as reliable as others. For example, if the sample was obtained by targeting

people on a door-to-door basis, that is more reliable than an online survey which will only be accessed by those who have the internet or who participate in such surveys.

Turning to a more involved inquiry, how reputable is the research institution? In analyzing any market research, the writer should always adhere to the safe principle that the reputation of the researcher(s) matters. Companies who conduct their own research and then broadcast it publicly are particularly suspect in this regard, but other researchers, such as private research companies, need to be assessed on the basis of their past affiliations and the accuracy of previous reports. The latter is easier to determine where more than one institution has performed research on the same target market. It may be surprising to the writer how divergent the results turned out to be in such cases.

The reader is advised to see Chapter 4, on the ethics of copywriting, in order to address questions as to the admissibility or otherwise of research. Some clients may or may not approve of the use of embarrassing facts or material in their advertising, while the results of sponsored research are always regarded with suspicion by neutral subject experts. Writers who are struggling with such issues should assess the sentiments expressed in the next chapter. In order to understand the target market better, market research is an important tool to the copywriter. Entities may conduct such research specifically in order to assist a marketing campaign, or may already exist as part of new product development.

## *Inquiries At Source*

These inquiries are those made by the writer where they desire to have information that is held only by the advertising entity, or where they do not trust that provided by their other sources. Copywriters are allowed to insist on access to privileged information, even though they may yet be denied such access. Exactly how they handle the information is discussed in Chapter 4, which deals with this. It is to be expected that a client will necessarily provide the copywriter with what they consider to be enough information at the outset of the project. However, where the writer deems more information to be necessary, they may direct their inquiry in one of several ways. Some methods are listed below:

- **E-mail** : The chance of success here is low. People do not always reply to e-mails, or they may reply only some time later, once the project deadline has passed. Only use this method if you are already acquainted with the recipient or if you have ample time to perform your research.
- **Telephone Conversations** : Not recommended. People are busy, and they may not be able to field such a call immediately, or they may not be amenable to the idea.
- **Interview** : This is more reliable, since the it is by appointment and the other person is aware of its purpose and content. If you conduct an interview, keep it as short as possible. Peoples' time is at a premium, and one or two questions which they experience as unnecessary or superficial will encourage them

to end the interview as quickly as possible.

- **Organizational Literature** : Feel free to request this at any time. It takes a matter of minutes to provide to you, and you can then spend your time perusing it at leisure, at no extra cost to the client. You should, however, evaluate it in the same way as any other material.

At all times, the copywriter should be available to the client. Proper, ongoing communication between the client and the writer is essential in ensuring that the final text is satisfactory to the former. All private information should be treated with the necessary respect. The acquisition and retention of such material is discussed in Chapter 4. It should also be mentioned that, at times, commercial clients may request information or facts to be treated or disseminated in a way which may seem inappropriate or deceptive to the writer. This, too, has been discussed under the heading of ethics.

# CHAPTER FOUR
*Copywriting Ethical Considerations*

Similar to any occupation or profession, copywriting is subject to certain ethical standards, which may or may not be enforced by law. Writers need to be aware of these issues, since the repercussions of non-observance may be severe, and extend beyond their work to their professional reputation. At times, they may even be liable to criminal prosecution or civil lawsuits.

### *Copyright*

This is a burning issue in the online environment at this time. Standard computer operating systems, such as Windows or Linux, make the wholesale copying and transmission of even massive volumes of text extremely easy. In a matter of minutes, a user can transfer an entire website onto another one, inclusive of all text and images.

Clients typically are opposed to this method and its underlying philosophy. In order to understand their attitude, one needs to be aware of how search engines operate. Search engines list many, many results for a search term. How they rank those results is extremely important to advertising entities, because the higher up in the rankings that they are, the more traffic they are likely to have on their sites. Attempts at establishing a higher ranking are known Search Engine Optimization (SEO), which is an entirely separate and established field of activity in the online economy.

Search engines assign greater importance to sites which contain original text and images. Sites which have been scraped (i.e. copied from elsewhere) rank lower in the results pages. It is therefore highly detrimental to a marketing campaign to make use of any copied or duplicate text or material at all, at any time, for any reason. Search engines will identify the oldest source of that material, assume that that is the original author, and rank it higher than the client's site in their results. The internet therefore penalizes writers who resort to such underhand tactics. Writers cannot simply duplicate or paste content. However, some clients will actually request the re-phrasing of existing text in such a way that it appears to be their own. This technique, which is known as "re-writing", is standard practice online, and is used where the client is trying to establish a better ranking in the search engine results without the generation of entirely new text. Yet even in such situations, the original text is usually the client's own, and they are merely trying to distribute it to another site.

Besides the search engines, programs such as Copyscape are able to determine whether a text is authentically original. At present, image recognition software is being introduced into search engine platforms, so the wholesale copying and duplication of images is not advisable either. Ultimately, the basic principle of autonomous text6 and image production should hold priority in the approach of any copywriter. Clients are not paying for second-hand material, and the target market may be alarmingly adept at detecting such work in the advertising that is presented to them. Besides, such considerations, the legal implications of copyright, trademarks and plagiarism need to be included in the copywriter's professional outlook. Corporate branding is an enormous industry, and marketers do not appreciate the hi-jacking or assimilation of their material into the campaigns of competitors, or even companies in other, unrelated industries. Litigation sometimes arises around this nettlesome issue, and some companies have attempted to patent entire words or phrases.

An experienced copywriter is aware that the creation and marketing of a successful slogan or brand logo is not easy. Millions of dollars might be spent on such material. Research, consultation and experimentation, all of which require ample financial and other resources, are required in the formulation and introduction to the market of a new corporate package. Holding a trademark on a slogan or emblem does not, therefore, merely entail the patent registration fee. Decades of operation in the industry, in conjunction with immense expenditure on marketing and customer relations, substantiate the prominence and success of that motto or emblem. Trademark litigation is about far more than a letterhead or the graphic designer's fees for a few days of work in the studio. Copywriters abuse the material of others at their peril. The same emphasis on uniqueness and proprietary ownership that applies to corporate branding applies equally to the text that the advertising entity has commissioned. It is their text, something that writers may not always understand or accept. Once the text has been sold to the client, the writer has no further rights in it and should not distribute or market it to other potential clients.

### *Accuracy of Information*

This issue has been alluded to in Chapter 2 on research methods. The accuracy of the information contained in the copy is not negotiable. Advertisers need to provide only reliable facts, statistics and product details. This is about more than mere administrative integrity, since there are two possible negative repercussions for advertises (and their writers) who do not do so.

Firstly, the legal environment in which marketing takes place doers not tolerate inaccurate advertising. It is extremely easy for members of the target market to institute complaints and action against enterprises who disregard this phenomenon. Some consumers develop severe irritation at misleading or unfounded facts and claims in marketing material, and they may make a point of notifying the authorities and pursuing corrective or prohibitive action against such advertisers. Even where no such action is taken, or is possible, however, the advertiser still stands to lose out if they resort to inaccurate material. Consumers do not only assess a product or service on the basis of its stated features or performance, but evaluate its performance and then make their conclusions. I|f they are unsatisfied with that performance, they may compare it to what the manufacturer or supplier has promised them. Sometimes, the discrepancy is not so significant as to provoke outrage, but where the consumer is unable to reconcile the advertised nature of the item with what they have experienced in practice, retributive measures are likely. Copywriters may deploy two tactics in circumventing this potential hazard. One is the subtle, or not so subtle, employment of language, in an attempt to attract attention and coerce a positive reaction in the target readership, without revealing the true nature of the product. An example would be the use of broad, undefined adjectives, such as "superior". The obvious question is: superior to what? The advertisement does not state the answer to that question, so it is impossible for the reader to question its veracity or for industry authorities to investigate or regulate the material. This is discussed more completely in Chapter 2.

The other safeguard is to ensure that information supplied by the client is authentic. Writers should use their discretion in this regard. Where they sense that data may be too contrived or extreme to be plausible, they should conduct some of their own research. If they ascertain that the information is not legitimate, they then have to decide as to how to approach the client concerning its suitability in the material. This is not always an easy dialog to maintain. Some clients may insist on the inclusion of data which are either contested or which are blatantly untrue. An example would be the health supplements that have developed into a sub-industry in the pharmaceutical industry, and which are typically marketed as producing absurd results in the health of their consumers. Weight loss of 100lb in two weeks? Through taking two tablets every day? Going from a barbell mass in the gym of 50lb to 250lb in one month? Really?

Writers need to determine at the outset whether they are prepared to accept a brief that entails this issue. The potential implication for their professional situation is that the advertising may be criticized or even banned, in which case they will be unable to present it in their portfolio of past work, or include it on their CV. On an ethical level, the nature of such material also precludes a wholesome approach to writing and publication.

### *Privacy of Information*

Client information is sometimes sensitive, in terms of its status in the industry. Where a client I introducing a new product, or they are supplying data on their internal operations, the writer needs to maintain absolute professional confidentiality. This may not seem to be so important where the specifications of the product are listed, since they will be made available to the target market anyway. Even statistics such as sales figures or performance measurements are not usually concealed. However, where more sensitive data are involved, such as market research or safety ratings, the copywriter needs to be very circumspect in how they present such information, if they present it at all. The primary question is as to how substantial the impact of the data is going to be on the reputation and image of the advertising entity. As an example, market share statistics can potentially cause some consumers to select or disregard a company as a service provider. If a company has only a 10% share of the target market, this may be interpreted by some customers as a negative aspect of that business, and they will avoid it. The prominence of advertising can actually create the impression that the advertiser has many more customers than they in fact do, so the writer should not reveal such data at any time. Advertising has the propensity to generate an impression in the target market that may be very different to the situation in reality, and the irresponsible exposure of salient facts can reverse that outcome, insofar as such concrete circumstances are not relevant to the quality of the product or service.

This emphasis on discretion extends to their entire professional and personal environments. Casually disclosed facts, no matter how insignificant they may seem to the writer, can cause havoc for the compromised advertiser. It may happen that a writer is made privy to sensitive data as part of their assignment, and if this is the case, they should manage the situation with the necessary maturity.

*Client Relations*

Managing relationships with clients I an integral aspect of the copywriter's profession, and requires more attention in this e-book. The points outlined here are general ones which may also have relevance in other areas of activity, and anyone who has significant experience in client management and corporate communication should easily be able to adapt their expertise to the writing environment.

To start with, the client needs to be communicated with promptly and in a transparent fashion. Writers should also be available at all times to their clients. Last-minute revisions, urgent briefs or mere discussion of delivered texts are important in the industry, and a writer who is reclusive or not available on a regular basis is likely to lose assignments and eventually have no clients. No-one is so talented, experienced or qualified that their capricious nature or bohemian approach to professional interactions will be tolerated. The fact that someone is a writer does not justify the attitude that they are an "artist" or that they should live a "rock 'n roll" lifestyle. Professional people, such as other writers, are not going to entertain that outlook. Professional writing can sometimes be very administrative, or mechanical, and professional discipline should be maintained in every aspect of the writer's operations. Many writers do not see themselves as artists and have no such pretensions. They never attempt purely creative texts either, yet they are massively successful at producing high quality copy. This is especially so in copywriting, which sometimes necessitates a creative mindset. The client may return the text several times, making such obscure comments as "it doesn't flow" or "it doesn't feel right". Writers need to be patient, and take time to discuss this feedback with the unsatisfied client. Usually, there are valid reasons why the client does not approve of the text, and it merely requires a little more conversation to extract those reasons from them, so that the writer is then able to improve the text.

Writers should also appreciate that clients may have immense stakes riding on the success of promotional material. Declining market share and industry rivalry can cause tortuous stress to competing enterprises, and the criticism of the client, which may seem harsh or even unreasonable, needs to be assessed in the context of that type of environment. Also, any operator in a media-based industry, especially the creative sectors, should be able to accept and process criticism in good grace, and apply it effectively in their future work. Fort their part, clients may also be guilty of malpractice, or of methods which obstruct the writer or the success of the project, whether inadvertently or otherwise, this has been touched on in Chapter 2. The brief should be discussed until the writer is absolutely sure about what the client expects from them./ A vacillating or indecisive client should be treated politely, but also with some sense of promptitude, since a missed deadline is blamed by default on the writer. Writers should also be especially cautious of clients who reject material for spurious, ill-defined or no apparent reason(s). Internet copywriters, in particular, are susceptible to this practice. If this happens, the writer should spend some time searching for their text at a later stage. They may be surprised to see that it is, in fact, in use, perhaps in a modified form.

Generally, though rejection should be accepted in a professional disposition. It is not always an indication of poor quality, but may be simply due to the capricious nature of the client or a misunderstood project description. Copywriting, especially, creates the opportunity for this to happen. Any creative material is liable to a certain degree of subjective assessment, and some clients simply cannot be satisfied, not matter how hard the writer tries, or only after several drafts have been submitted. Such clients will, however, appreciate the perseverance of the writer, and may reward them latter with future assignments. Another point to note is that the client should be regarded as the subject expert. If they express the opinion that material is not suitable for the target market, the writer should not argue with that, unless they have established solid grounds on which to do so, or they are genuinely more experienced in addressing the target audience than the client. Usually, however, clients know their customers better than anyone else, and their feedback, no matter how acerbic or critical, is priceless in shaping the ideal text.

### *Personal Philosophy*

The primary requirement in the industry is that, where a writer genuinely believes that they are unable to be associated with an enterprise or cause, or product, they state that issue as soon as possible, and reject the brief entirely, so that the client is able to pursue the services of another writer. Proselytization, though, is not within the ambit of the copywriter, and they should not attempt to level an assault on the client through persistent unsolicited communication or disparaging remarks.

It is, however, possible to express one's personal beliefs in a professional manner, and usually where a writer opts to take that route, they have the support of a known and substantial community within the industry. At times, the promotion of such beliefs or principles may even attract the support of other writers and clients, and serve to enhance the writer's reputation and enlarge their client base.

## *Summary*

The mass distribution and production of text that has been enabled by the internet has provided even ordinary,m small-scale writers with an immense potential audience. Anything uploaded onto the internet is totally public, and totally exposed to scrutiny and criticism. It is also open to investigation by l;aw enforcement. Printed matter, too, eventually arrives online and can be assessed in the same way. It therefore behoves the writer to remain sensitive to the issues raised in this chapter at all times, and to produce their texts in a safe and sensible manner. The possibility of criminal sanction or civil litigation may not serve as a deterrent to many people, since they may assume that their work is too poorly regarded or that its audience is too insignificant to merit a more cautious attitude about such measures.

Their approach may yet prove destructive to their ambitions as writers. First, the internet provides resources which make the detection and publicism of plagiarism extremely easy. There are programs available, such as Copyscape, and the search engines also allow the identification of matching text to a limited degree. Subject experts are extremely well versed in the literature of their fields. Any text that arrives in their in-box or which they encounter in other media is then automatically compared to their existing base of reading. They are easily able to determine identical wording, or similar sentiments, especially in subject areas where cutting-edge research is taking place or there are conflicting viewpoints.

Writers who resort to unethical tactics are actively working towards the destruction oft heir reputations and future client relationships. Plagiarism, once detected, is impossible to disprove, and no excuses are accepted. The assertion that he culpable writer was unaware of the existing text or that they "read it somewhere, but they couldn't remember where, so they used it anyway" do not alleviate guilt, and merely serve to reinforce the perception of that writer as uninformed, lazy, or incompetent. Once a professional writer is associated with plagiarism, it is extremely hard for them to lose that connotation, and they may experience a substantial or even complete deterioration of their writing activities. No-one will use them. So, while the technical, legal consequences may not seem palpable, the professional implications of unethical writing practices are too serious to ignore, and the writer who engages in such practices probably does not appreciate the importance of their task or the possibilities that it enables. Usually, though, writers who use such methods are substandard in some way. They either do not have the ability to produce satisfactory texts, such as where they are writing in a second language, or they have not allowed enough time for proper research. In some instances, their use of language is simply too poor to meet the demands of a professional writing task, or they have accepted a brief that they genuinely are unable to satisfy due to its excessively technical or scientific nature. Even if this description does not apply to them, people will suspect that it does as a matter of course, and the plagiarist will be at a disadvantage in securing future assignments or marketing their services. A simple example in illustration of this point is the recent experience of the author of this e-book, in which an individual in another country attempted to initiate a suspected phishing exercise targeting the latter. Phishing is the illegal, disguised extraction of personal information from another internet user, by infiltrating their PC. The phisher, who purported to be an online pen-pal, supplied various personal details (and even supposed photos of themselves) via e-mail.

When this author requested that they describe their home city of Accra, in Ghana, their response was to copy and paste informative text from an online source. The text, which was in impeccable English, was in stark contrast to the person's usual obviously deficient use of the

English language. Needless to say, the correspondence was abandoned. Not only was the pasted text easy to locate on its home site, but the discrepancy in writing styles was so vast as to be highly suspicious, and the "pen-pal" was reported to local law enforcement.

Writers who engage in plagiarism expose themselves to the possibility of eliciting a similar response and should not be tolerated under any circumstances by other operators in the text industry. The primary aim of sales copy is to generate a return on the advertising material. The material needs to achieve an outcome, such as increased market share or higher sales. Unfortunately, some advertisers are so obsessed with this priority that they progressively discard any sense of ethics or standards of legitimacy until their advertising is, in reality, of no use, because only the most desperate, uninformed or naive consumers would take it seriously, and only in a single instance, after which they would reject the advertiser's market offering with disgust and rue the day that they ever considered it in the first place. The underlying proportion in advertising copy is that, the more ethical and legitimate it is, the more easily it accesses the target market, and it is therefore more effective.

# CHAPTER FIVE
*Resources and Support For Copywriting*

Aspiring copywriters, and those already established in the trade, may realize that the necessary skills and experience take time to acquire. Alternatively, an advertiser may be trying to determine why their copy is not generating the volume of sales that they intended it to. This is particularly so where the advertiser is producing their own copy, which some may attempt given the rates that agencies or professional writers sometimes charge. Professional writing is an industry, and like any other, its is populated by operators with varying levels of expertise and commercial success. Some of them are highly qualified, and have been associated with prestigious campaigns in the past, while others are lesser known or non-descript and ply their trade for smaller enterprises and secondary role-players in their respective sectors of activity. Yet the temptation is always there to produce one's own copy, since some may feel that writing is something everyone is capable of, and that they possess superior brand knowledge or target market familiarity to an outside writer who represents them with a hefty invoice on delivery of the text. This chapter is aimed at those who are trying to write their own copy. Agencies, established writers and other critics may not discover anything new or important in these paragraphs, which are intended to serve merely as guidance for those who are new to the industry or who are trying to understand and master a specific writing challenge or (negative) professional interaction.

### *Industry Support*

Other than what they manage to source for themselves, the industry does not provide practical support in terms of technical skill or the management of briefs. Industry authorities have very little, if any, relevance, since there is no standardization of qualifications or ideal CV. Online copy is produced in countries as far away as India and Pakistan, by speakers of other home languages than the one they write in.

The basic principle of copyright still holds, though, and should never be ignored. Legal authorities, the more general ones, can and will investigate and intervene if they deem the offense to be serious enough. The internet makes the detection of plagiarism easy, so while the prosecution of individual offenders I not possible where they are geographically too remote to be affected by it, their nefarious strategy can be thwarted nonetheless. On a broader level, patent law is applicable to marketing material and specialist attorneys are able to institute steps to eliminate offensive copy from the market. As to professional affiliations, these are not generally recognized, and as such it is of no use to recommend any. Some writers may advertise that they are qualified at tertiary level, and this is possibly to their advantage, but the ultimate test of their skill is in their past work, and the measure of success that it has achieved, and this is a concept that applies to anyone else in the industry.

### *Writing Aids & Guidance*

Nowadays, literacy is not seen as exceptional or especially praiseworthy. Everyone learns to read and write at school (hopefully). However, it is a fact of life that some people are more able than others in this sphere of human activity. Some people readily admit to this, while others are more reserved about their (perceived) limited ability, and it is a source of embarrassment to them. Nevertheless, writing, especially strategic text production (such as sales copy) is an area of expertise that requires some form of training and practice to become proficient in. the excuse that someone has always been useless at writing, or that they don't have a wide vocabulary, is not necessarily so persuasive where they have extensive product knowledge or they have many years of experience in dealing with the target market. What is not trainable, though, is the artistic ability of some writers. They are able to produce incisive, notable texts on a regular basis, and about a vast range of subjects. This ability to use language effectively, regardless of the identity of the target reader or the nature of the subject matter, is a indeed a talent, and the aspiring writer needs to assess and accept their own innate level of ability. At the same time, the quality of copy (or its artistry) is not always the reason why it is so successful. Some writers have access to high-profile briefs and clients purely through their industry network of contacts or their previous acclaim. They command large fees and they write for impressive institutions. Yet their work is not superior by default. In some instances, one is brought to ponder how copy was passed for publication at all, even that which is used by major enterprises in the economy.

The primary objective of generating interest and sales should always be remembered. The writer then shapes their text around what is going to work in each specific situation. This is similar to sports players. There are those players who supporters believe should not be in the team, but are merely there through their connections in the sport, or due to prior achievements in years gone by, or because they are new in the industry and they have not yet proven their competence (or lack thereof). Then there are those who regularly deliver solid performances and contribute to the team's success. But the genuinely special players, the ones whose jerseys the kids beg their parents for in the clothing stores, are the ones who, time and again, come up with a scintillating or unconventional play that no-one else though of or anticipated and which is not found in any coaching manual.

The last type of player, the superstar, is the true genius in the industry. But they are a tiny minority. They set standards and make headlines, but they are extremely costly, and largely unavailable to ordinary clients who need more mundane, yet equally important, copy.

Most writers are like the second type of player, who are reliable in their output, serve the need they are hired to, and establish their position over a period of time and consistent performance. The first type, namely the non-functioning ones or the rookies who never had the expertise to start with, soon disappear as clients reject their texts or they lose interest in a task that they realize (or persuade themselves) is beyond their (present) ability. There is no need for the aspiring copywriter to use the superstars as their examples. It is not advisable to pay too much attention to other peoples' work, because you do not know wheat their brief was, or to be daunted by their creativity. Shaping the artistry to suit the task at hand, such as increasing sales, is the true objective in copywriting, and those who prefer to produce absolutely artistic texts should concern themselves with novels and poetry. A very successful piece of copy is not necessarily very creative, and vice versa. It doesn't take a Leonardo da Vinci to design a skyscraper, even though the successful architect is unable to paint the Mona Lisa. In some cases, the blueprint provided by the supreme artist is rejected anyway, since it is not workable. For those seeking further reading or guidance on how to write, there are several sources. These are listed below:

### 1. *The Internet*

The Internet is a useful starting point in researching writing and writing techniques. There is a large amount of material available on how to write, how to write excellent content, and how to make sure that your copy generates interest or increases traffic to your site.

Given that there is so much advice available, the writer needs to be very discerning in how they approach it. They may not agree with some commentators, and they may also encounter the phenomenon of proprietary commentary, i.e. copywriters who have published texts on the subject and who believe that their opinion is so valuable as to be worth money to other people. In selecting which advice to adhere to, or which prominent writers to observe as role models, the writer needs to be able to reconcile their chosen sources with the nature of the work that they are (usually) engaged in. the choice of role model should preferably be industry specific, as should the guidelines that they decide to pursue.

## 2. Literature On Style

Language academics have a penchant for producing such works. These are books on how to use language, and not only use it, but to do so correctly, or even in strategic ways. These books offer a host of insights in this topic, and are useful; to those who have realized that their use of language is too ordinary or limited to achieve success in the copywriting environment. There is no recommended method o choosing an author or work to use for this purpose. What is important is that the chosen text is as recent as possible, and that it discusses the language that the writer is operating in. This is especially significant in the use of English, because clients typically insist on a certain variation of English, such as US or British. There are vast differences between the two, not only in mere spelling, and the writer should be aware of this issue and be able to operate equally well in either.

### 3. Job Shadowing

This is a standard practice in many industries, and allows new entrants or aspiring participants the opportunity to observe and imitate what existing role-players do on a daily basis. However, in terms of improving one's writing skills, this is not likely to be a productive exercise. It should serve to provide a greater understanding of client relations, and how to manage and execute a brief administratively. It may also give some insight into how professional writers manage the creative exercise, or apportion their time and conduct their research. Possible job shadowing venues would be advertising agencies and publishers. Anyone who is interested in this option should not hesitate to contact such organizations to arrange the shadowing.

# CONCLUSION

The assumption that copywriting is the preserve of bohemian arts graduates with unkempt hair and floral shirts should be abandoned. It is hoped that this book has gone some way towards achieving that outcome. Copywriter do not usually have poor personal hygiene or a substance abuse habit, and the elimination of that impression is important in persuading subject experts or people with extensive industry experience that they are also able to approach the target market textually, sometimes better so than others. With appropriate training and consistent application, the re are various skills in writing than can be mastered, and some very successful copywriters did not reach that level of expertise in the absence of outside assistance or education.

For those who desire to start their own writing career, or who need to engage in the activity due to the needs of their own commercial enterprises, this book should provide encouragement and a basic understanding of the issues at play, as well as some of the techniques that are useful or, at least, available, depending on the actual situation

## Conclusion

in which the writer is operating. In time, those who persevere may be surprised at how easily they produce texts they once thought only others were able to. Ultimately, copywriting requires individual input. The most successful advertisements either contain an element of creative genius, or extremely intelligent manipulation of existing target market sentiment or current events. This is not an ability that is limited to writing, or any other sphere of activity, and the approach should always be one of enthusiasm and open-mindedness at the outset.

We really hope that the information provided in this book was valuable to you and that it over delivered on your expectations. If for any reason you are not satisfied with your purchase, or if you have any comments or feedback you would like to share with us directly, please reach us at clydebankpublishing@gmail.com.

# PREVIEW OF
*Business Plan Writing Guide :*
*How To Write A Successful & Sustainable Business Plan In Under 3 Hours*
## By : Devon Wilcox

*Chapter 1 : Before You Begin*

Before you get into the actual writing of your business plan, it's important to understand all those questions you probably have about your business plan like, do you actually need one, why you need one, how long it should be, and when you should write it. So let's take a few minutes to answer all those questions before we dive into the actual writing of your business plan.

*Who Needs a Business Plan?*

This is kind of a trick question, because everyone needs a business plan. If you are going into any type of business, whether it's a new startup company that's just venturing out, or an established business that's looking to expand; a business plan is an absolute necessity. You will even find that as a business owner, the business plan that you create in the beginning is helpful all through out your company's existence. Your plan only grows and develops as your company grows and develops.

## Why Write a Business Plan?

First and foremost, research has shown that you are two and half times more likely to actually go into business if you take the time to write a business plan. With that in mind, it's probably worth writing a business plan. So why is this statistic true? Researchers believe that those who take the time to write business plans have proven that they are willing to take the extra steps to make running a business work. Business plans are used for a variety of reasons, but one of their main purposes is to show potential investors your overall goals and strategies for your business.

Investors like to see all of your research in one neat and tidy document. They also like to see that you've done your research and have the ability to follow through with that research. It shows that you can take all of your ideas and the research that you have done prior to talking with investors and put it down on paper in a nice, concise format. Many business owners will tell you that writing a business plan was essential for them, because it helped them organize their thoughts before they talked to investors and before they made any major business decisions. Business plans are a great tool to get you thinking about all the aspects of your business, which is one of reasons they are so valuable to write. You'll think about your marketing strategy and your finances, as well as your start-up costs and your business management and organization. Thinking through all of these individual details as you get started will take your big ideas and focus them into very specific areas.

Overall writing a business plan is a vital tool for getting started with your business. It's a proven statistic for getting your business off the ground, and even required by many investors, so take the time to make sure your business plan is professional and done well.

### When Should I Write My Business Plan?

Business plans are the tool that you use to organize your business. They are a way for you to take everything that's floating around in your head and organize it into one place. For many people, it's a way to get key investors on board with your business, but your business plan is much more than that. Remember that you will need to employ several people other than yourself, so your business plan can help to recruit those key employees to work for you. So when should you write your business plan? Before you really get started doing any of those things, you'll need a business plan. Before you talk to investors, you are going to need a business plan. Before you are able to recruit employees to your business you will need a business plan.

You can also use your business plan to watch how your business progresses through out the first weeks, months and years. If you project that your company will have certain profits by the end of the first quarter, you can check those things. A business plan only works if it was created prior to your business starting its operations.

## How Long Should My Business Plan Be?

Overall business plans should be short and too the point. They shouldn't be overly wordy and should be straightforward. Investors and possible employees don't want to waste incredible amounts of time reading through long documents, but they are interested in what you have to say, so make every sentence and every word count. Here are a few tips to making your business plan as effective as possible:

- **Consider using shorter sentences.** Longer sentences are okay, but only if you really want to use them for a specific meaning. People may be reading your business plan while on the phone, or while doing other things. They may also just skim through your business plan. Don't take it personal, it's just the way it is, and if your sentences are too long or complicated, they won't pick up on key things you want to get across.

- **Use common language.** Avoid using acronyms, jargon or other words that only people in your field would know. If you feel that you need to, explain them briefly, so your reader can understand what it means. You can't always assume that your readers know the same things that you do.

- **Use bullet points for lists.** They will help your readers stay focused on what you are trying to get across and help to emphasize the most important things. They can also easily go back and find information that was important or something that they want to reference again after reading through your business plan. When you have bullet points, don't just list things without giving an explanation. There is nothing more frustrating to a reader than to have a list, but no explanation to accompany the list. Make sure everything on your list is adequately explained, so your reader isn't left with questions.

- **Keep it short.** The average length of a business plan today is around forty pages. You will have around 20-30 pages of regular text for all the parts of your business plan and then around ten pages of appendices. We will explain what all those entail later, but it's important to note that if your business plan ends up more than 40 pages, you should probably go back and see where you can cut back and summarize pieces better.

- **Add graphics and visuals.** Consider adding graphics or pictures of your product, location, menus, floor plans, logos, etc. All of these can be very useful in your business plan. You may find that when you add in lots of graphics to your business plan, it can add significant length to your document. If that happens don't fret, you can still use the 40 rule; just see how it measures without the graphics. Don't shy away from adding in graphics just because it lengthens your business plan. Charts can do the same thing. Think of bar graphs or pie charts that can enhance the market comparisons or profit margins you are projecting. These visuals can add valuable and help legitimize your business plan.

- **Choose your font wisely.** Perhaps this goes without saying, but use a very readable font that is standard, even though they are very boring. You can change the font for your headings, but stick to only two fonts for your whole document. Keep it simple.
- **Use spellcheck and proofread.** If grammar and punctuation aren't your strong point, have a friend or colleague do you a favor. Make sure to double-check all your numbers, too. This is something that a friend proofreading can't check, so that's your responsibility! The last thing you want is to be embarrassed when your figures don't add up for an investor.

Hopefully we've talked through some of your initial questions about business plans. It's important that you feel confident about writing your business before you get started.

## *Chapter 2 : Do Your Homework*

Before you get started writing your own business plan, there's some homework of your own that you'll have to do. This is the part where you have to do your research and prepare your research to outline your goals and objectives. Here are some important pieces to research through as you do your homework.

### *Research Your Potential Markets*

This is the research where you start to think and analyze who is going to actually use the products and/or services that you are going to be offering. This shouldn't be you just guessing or thinking through the potential market either. You should actually put your feet on the pavement and talk to potential customers and ask them questions. Conduct real interviews, collect data, and ask questions of people that you think you might actually be selling to.

One of the most important questions to ask yourself when you start is to consider if there is a market for your product or service in your area. Hopefully the answer to this question is yes; otherwise, you're in trouble. Think outside the box, because usually with a little creativity there is a market for just about anything, it just needs to be presented in the right way and marketed well. If you truly believe there isn't a market for your product in your area, and you're passionate about opening your business, you'll have to consider relocating to an area where there is a market for your product or service.

After you have determined that there is a market for your product or service, you will continue to ask further follow-up questions. Ask questions about age groups, gender, ethnicities, economic populations, etc. After analyzing those types of questions think about if your potential customers live in certain neighborhoods or certain areas of town more than others. Are you targeting kids or adults? Compile this data together so you can easily access the data later when you need to for your business plan. You can collect the data all yourself, but sometimes it's better if the data is collected by someone else, because it is coming from an outside source, so it is unbiased. When you use a secondary source other than yourself, sometimes people are more willing to be honest instead of just telling you what they think you want to hear.

Regardless of how you choose to do your market research, this is one of the most important pieces of research. You will learn invaluable information that will guide you through the rest of the business planning process. Take your time and make sure you research your potential markets well and in great detail.

### *Determine Potential Market Size*

When you first start out, you probably have big dreams of becoming extremely successful. Those dreams aren't impossible, and you should dream big, but you've got to start small. Along with analyzing your market, you need to consider your market size and how many potential customers you have. You might start out thinking that you have hundreds of thousands of potential customers, but that's probably a little out of your reach at the beginning. Think of it this way. You've invented a new line of toothpaste – a product that everyone uses, right? So potentially your market size could be the entire population of the world. That seems crazy and unthinkable now but consider popular toothpaste brands that really do market to the entire world – they had to start somewhere, right? It is possible to get there, but you need to start with a smaller market size, first and then work your way up to larger market sizes.

So maybe start with toothpaste that specifically targets one group of people, like children, toddlers, people with dentures, etc. After you've narrowed your market size you can start to ask yourself more specific questions about that market group. By asking yourself these questions and other questions similar to these, you can begin to learn where you fit in your market.

- How many toddlers need toothpaste in any given community?
- How many people with dentures currently live in the US?
- How much toothpaste do people go use in a month or a year?
- Who else are you competing against in the toothpaste market?

### *What Do You Need to Get Started?*

This is basically sitting down and making a list of things you need to get yourself up and running as a company. Some of the things you need are simple and easy to obtain, like office supplies and computers, while others are much more complicated, like employees and product designs. At this point, don't be afraid to make the list as detailed as you need, not leaving anything out. You'll obviously need plenty of tangible things for your business to get off the ground, but there are plenty of intangible things, too, like market research and potential customers to make it all come together.

This is the time for you to really think through every step that needs to take place in order for your company to launch and all the things that are standing in the way of that happening, down to the last paper clip (okay, maybe that's a little bit of an exaggeration, but you get the point).

### *Make Product Samples*

Potential investors want to see the product or products they are investing in, so you'll need to have wonderful product samples to show-off when you "pitch" your business plan to them. Likewise if you are offering a service instead of a product, be prepared to somehow demonstrate your service to them as well, like through a video demonstration. If you are opening a restaurant, invite potential investors for lunch and serve them a few dishes that will be on the menu. There are ample ways to show investors your products and services even if it isn't something they can't hold in their hands. In addition, future employees will also be interested to see product samples and services as well. You will need to show them that yours is a company worth putting their time and effort into in order to convince them to work for you. You are trying to convince these employees that your company is going to be successful, and they aren't going to be out looking for work in six months time. They also need to be excited about your product and services. They need to be selling the product as much as you are. If they are excited about the company it will show in their daily work habits and their dedication to the company.

Initially your product samples may have been something you produced in your garage, made with scraps of wood or pieces of junk metal. Although it may work great, you want a product sample that says "wow" when you pull it out of the box. It should be attractive and flashy. Take your initial model and dress it up a little to make it "shock" and "awe" your audience.

### *Find Possible Locations to Rent/Buy*

It's time to go location hunting. Although you may not actually be renting out a space for a few months or more, you need to research out what type of space you need, and the only way you'll be able to do that is by actually walking in some and seeing what you can get and how much they cost.

You will need to contact a real estate broker and have him or her walk you through several available retail spaces in neighborhoods that you are interested in opening up your business. Because you have already done your market research, you know the neighborhoods you are most interested in renting your business. Keep accurate records of all the places you see, so you know how much each place costs, the square footage, pictures, etc. Ultimately, you will learn quickly what you can get for your money in each of your chosen neighborhoods and how that will affect your decisions. It will give you a good idea of an estimated cost of how much you are going to need monthly to rent your location.

Rarely do businesses buy a location for their business, but it does happen (mostly when you find a steal of deal, or the perfect location). If you are interested in buying a location for your business, you can speak to your real estate broker about locations to buy as well. You will just need to factor that into your start-up costs.

### *Figure Out Start-up Costs*

Start-up costs aren't going to be pretty. This number will probably shock you in the beginning, but there are a couple of things to keep in mind. First, sit down and make a list of everything you need to get your business going. This is different from the list you made earlier, because this list only includes the things that cost money (it doesn't include the market research, the potential customers, etc.) Everything from the cash register and computers, to the industrial kitchen equipment and tables will need to be factored into the start-up costs.

If you are starting from nothing, you'll need to think about painting the walls, light fixtures, etc. However, at the same time, be reasonable and conservative. Instead of going for the light fixtures that cost two hundred dollars a piece, see if you can find something more reasonable and cheaper. You don't have to find something at a thrift store, but just maybe something more reasonably priced.

At the beginning, cover the basics or the most important things and then down the road when you are turning a good profit you can consider adding a few of the more expensive extras. Remember that right now you are just trying to get started, so don't go over the top. Do your research and see where you can find the best prices for things. There are plenty of places online that offer discounts for ordering in bulk. Since you will probably be ordering things in higher quantities, see if you can find those kinds of websites or stores. Build relationships with other local businesses that might offer your discounts if you buy their products in bulk as well. Here are a few things to remember when factoring in your start-up costs, but of course there could be many more depending on your situation:

- Rent
- Utilities
- Salaries for Employees
- Equipment
- Maintenance for Equipment
- Other Supplies
- Legal Licenses or Permits
- Marketing and Promotion

Potential investors will want to see that you have researched and thought through your start-up costs, down to the very last paperclip (this time, yes, even the paperclips). Make an organized chart breaking down each part of your start-up costs so your investors can see how the money will be divided. It is helpful for them because this way they can see exact numbers linked to specific expenses. If you can break it down and show them where each dollar is going to be spent, the more eager they will be to finance you. If you are struggling to get started with you start-up costs, there are free online calculator tools that help to breakdown your costs for the first six months.

## Who Are Your Potential Investors?

You might have the best idea for a business in the world, but without the backing of a bank or a wealthy investor(s), you aren't ever going to reach a single customer. People don't lend money just because you are a nice person or even because you have a good idea. There are actually specific guidelines that you have to meet in order for them to lend you money. Obviously if your idea is a good one, then you are well on your way to meeting the guidelines, but you'll have to take it just a little further in order to secure yourself the loan and make your dream of owning a business a reality. Banks and other lenders generally look at a potential business' capital, capacity, collateral, conditions, and character (the 5C's of lending), in order to determine whether or not they will lend to it. So let's talk about what each of these 5C's mean to you, so you can prepare yourself and make sure you are ready when you walk into the bank to talk with potential investors about your business.

- **Capital** : This is basically what other sources of income you have to repay the loan, other than the business you are trying to open. The bank wants to know if you lose your job, the business goes under, etc. are there other ways of repayment for the loan, like investments, savings, assets, etc.

- **Capacity** : The bank will want to know how you handle debt and whether you can manage this new debt with your current income. They will judge this debt against any current debt you have – this called debt-to-income ratio. They may judge this based on your former employment and any former debt you may have had and how you handled paying it off.

- **Collateral** : This only applies if you are applying for a secured loan. A secured loan means that you are placing something as collateral against the loan. Think of an auto loan or a home equity loan. When you have those loans, there is a car or a house that the bank has as collateral against the loan. So if you don't pay the loan back, the bank can come and take the car or house back. If you apply for a secured loan, you are offering something as collateral against the loan or at least part of the loan.

- **Conditions** : The bank can ask how you plan to use the money they are loaning you. This can be anything from very general to very specific, so be prepared to answer for every dollar you are asking for. If you plan to purchase a vehicle for your business, they may want to know, and they may want to inspect the vehicle in order to approve the loan. A loan officer may be assigned to you and may place very specific "conditions" on your loan that you have to follow in order for the loan to be approved.

- **Character** : This is also sometimes called Credit History instead of character, because the bank will pull your credit report and go over it will a fine tooth comb. They will want to know every detail of your credit history and your approval on your loan will be based widely on how your credit history looks to them. Have you defaulted on a loan before? Be prepared to defend yourself and then hope for the best. Banks don't like to see that, and they won't look highly on someone who has defaulted before, because your track record is against you. Luckily credit history does improve with time and if you defaulted years ago, it may not show up now.

If you are interested in seeing your credit score before you go to the bank, you can check your credit score for free. There are many imposter website online, so be wary of giving your personal information to just any website, but TransUnion, Equifax and Experian (the three credit report agencies) are required by law to give you a free credit report once every twelve months. Obviously it's only once a year, but you can check your score for free and there is no sign up for a week and cancel or get charged fees attached like most websites out there. If you are interested in seeing your scores, there are websites that provide your credit score for free.

Finding your potential investors and making sure that you are prepared with all the information you need to win them over is the key to getting your financing. Without financing, you obviously won't have a business, so making sure you're prepared and ready for their questions with product samples and a great business plan is the key to success.

Researching isn't the easiest thing, nor is it always the most fun, but it is vital to the success of your business plan. Now that you've done your research and you're prepared with all the right strategies, you are ready to start writing your actual business plan.

# ABOUT CLYDEBANK BUSINESS

ClydeBank Business is a division of the multimedia-publishing firm ClydeBank Media LLC. ClydeBank Media's goal is to provide affordable, accessible information to a global market through different forms of media such as eBooks, paperback books and audio books. Company divisions are based on subject matter, each consisting of a dedicated team of researchers, writers, editors and designers.

The Business division of ClydeBank Media is composed of contributors who are experts in their given disciplines. Contributors originate from diverse areas of the world to guarantee the presented information fosters a global perspective.

Contributors have multiple years of experience in successfully starting and operating online and offline businesses, marketing and sales, economics, management methodology and systems, business consulting, manufacturing efficiency and many other areas of discipline.

For more information, please visit us at :

www.clydebankmedia.com

or contact us at :

info@clydebankmedia.com

# MORE BY CLYDEBANK BUSINESS

**Etsy Business For Beginners**

*How To Build & Promote A Profitable Etsy Business*

Visit : http://bit.ly/etsy_business

**Agile Project Management QuickStart Guide**

*A Simplified Beginners Guide To Agile Project Management*

Visit : bit.ly/agile_quickstart

**Scrum QuickStart Guide**

*A Simplified Beginners Guide To Mastering Scrum*

Visit : bit.ly/scrumguide1

**Agile Project Management & Scrum Box Set**

*Agile Project Management QuickStart Guide*
*& Scrum QuickStart Guide*

Visit : bit.ly/agileprojectmana

**Lean Six Sigma QuickStart Guide**

*A Simplified Beginners Guide To Lean Six Sigma*

Visit : bit.ly/lean-sixsigma

## Project Management For Beginners

*Proven Project Management Methods To Complete Projects With Time & Money To Spare*

Visit : bit.ly/project_success

## Business Plan Writing Guide

*How To Write A Successful & Sustainable Business Plan In Under 3 Hours*

Visit : bit.ly/BusinessPlanWriting

## Copywriting Mastery

*Exactly How To Become A Professional Copywriting Expert & Create Content That Gets Attention & Sells*

Visit : bit.ly/CopywritingMastery

## 3D Printing Business

*How To Get Rich From Home With 3D Printing*

Visit : bit.ly/3dprinting_rich

## eBay Business For Beginners

*Exactly How I Make A Six Figure Income With My eBay Business And Why It Is Easier Than You Think*

Visit : bit.ly/ebay_rich

**Etsy Business For Beginners**

*How To Build & Promote A Profitable Etsy Business*

Visit : bit.ly/etsy_business

**Etsy & eBay Business Box Set**

*Etsy Business For Beginners & eBay Business For Beginners*

Visit : bit.ly/ebay_etsy

# GET A FREE CLYDEBANK MEDIA AUDIOBOOK + 30 DAY FREE TRIAL TO AUDIBLE.COM

## GET TITLES LIKE THIS ABSOLUTELY FREE:

- Business Plan Writing Guide
- ITIL for Beginners
- Stock Options for Beginners
- Scrum Quickstart Guide
- Project Management for Beginners
- 3D Printing Business

- LLC Quickstart Guide
- Lean Six Sigma Quickstart Guide
- Growing Marijuana for Beginners
- Social Security Simplified
- Medicare Simplified
- and more!

## TO SIGN UP & GET YOUR FREE AUDIOBOOK, VISIT:
www.clydebankmedia.com/audible-trial

Made in the USA
Lexington, KY
25 July 2018